RUBANK EDUCATIONAL LIBRARY No. 108

Selected Studies

Advanced Etudes, Scales and Arpeggios in All Major and All Minor Keys

CORNET OR TRUMPET

by H. Voxman

ADVANCED ETUDES

SCALES AND ARPEGGIOS

SPECIAL STUDIES

RUBANK®

HAL•LEONARD® CORPORATION
7777 W. BLUEMOUND RD. P.O. BOX 13819 MILWAUKEE, WI 53213

C Major

GALLAY

BÖHME

Alla breve

A Minor

GALLAY

Andante non troppo lento

Alla Polacca

BÖHME

F Major

PIETZSCH
(adapted)

DUHEM

Adagio cantabile

D Minor

BÖHME

Andante

Allegro maestoso

G Major

Larghetto cantabile

Allegro grotesco

E Minor

Valse, lentamente

BÖHME

Allegro moderato

Bb Major

GATTI

Allegro marziale

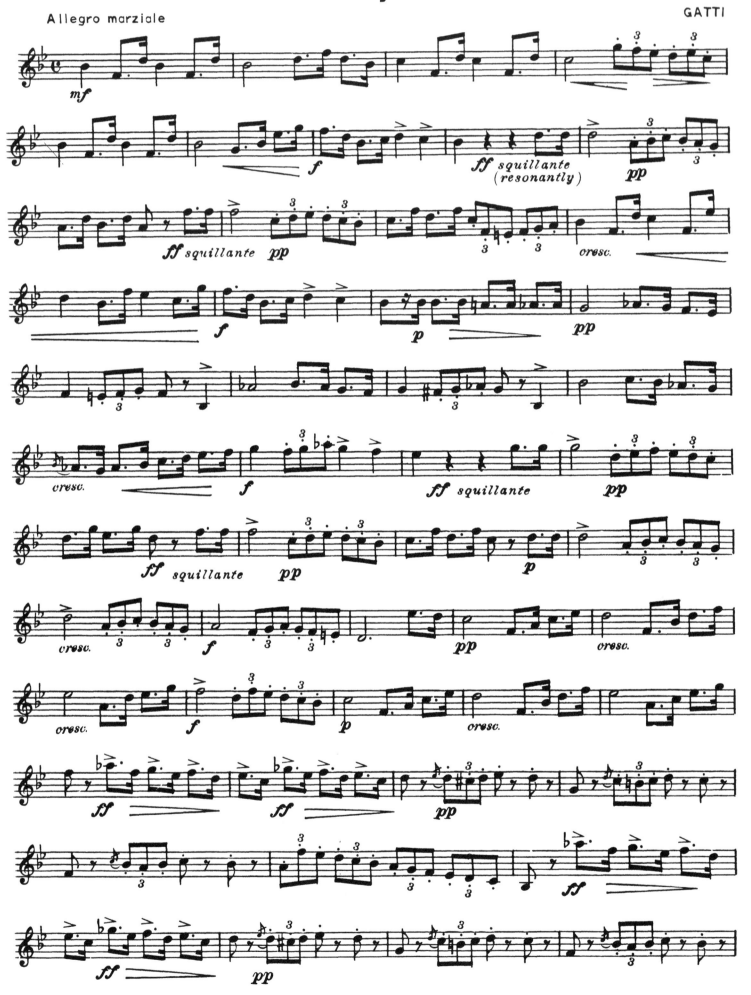

BÖHME

Vivace

G Minor

BÖHME

Lento (in 8)

GATTI

Allegretto affettuoso

D Major

BÖHME

Largo cantabile

GATTI

B Minor

GATTI

Allegretto grazioso

FEDOROW

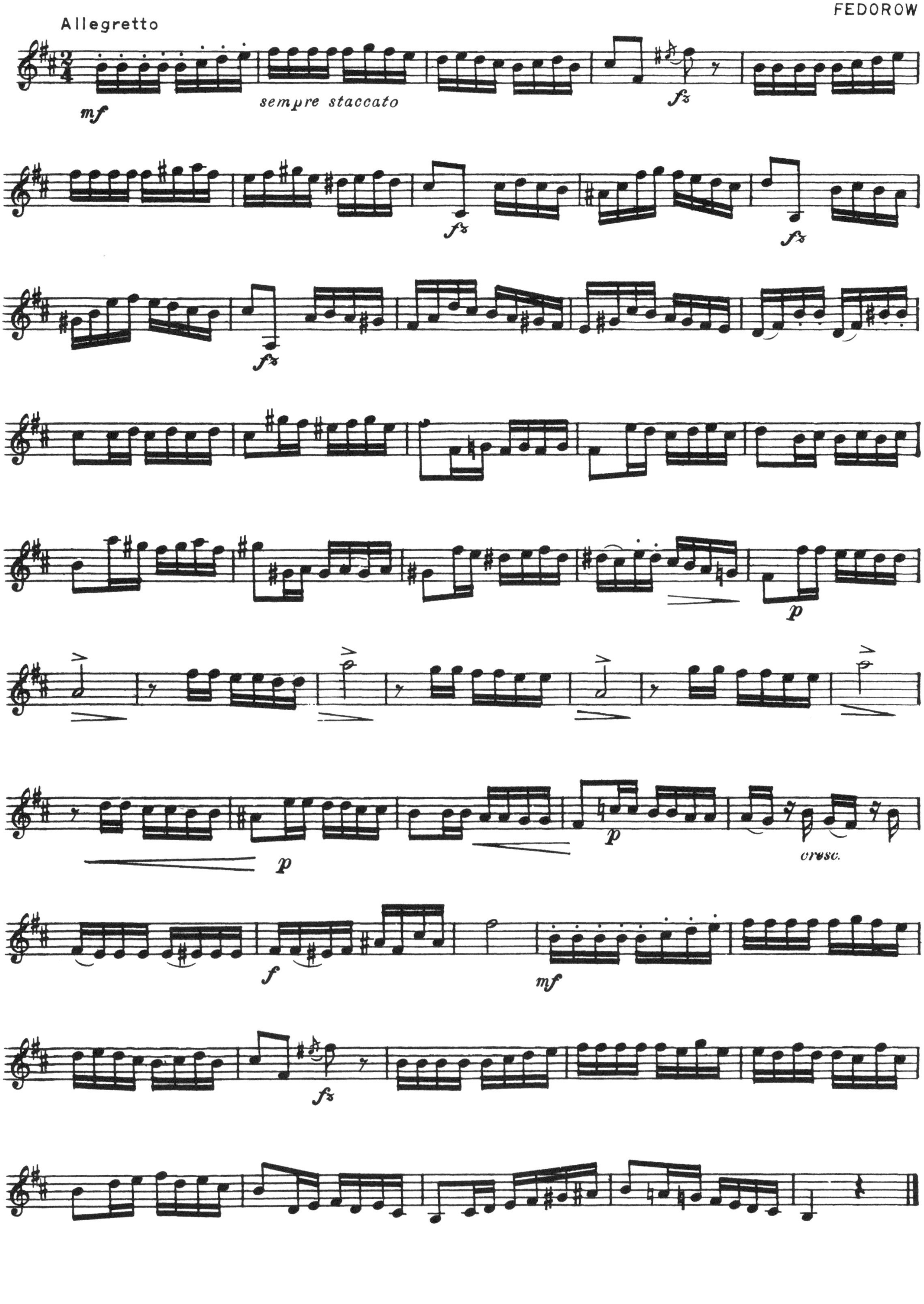

E♭ Major

PIETZSCH

ST. JACOME

Maestoso

C Minor

CAPRICCIO

ST. JACOME

Allegretto

BÖHME

p *legére*

A Major

Tempo di Polacca

FEDOROW

Fine   *p dolce*

D.C. al Fine

Allegretto

BÖHME

F♯ Minor

BÖHME

A♭ Major

DUHEM

Allegro non troppo

F Minor

BAGANTZ

Moderato

GATTI

E Major

FEDOROW

Allegro con moto

FEDOROW

C# Minor

GATTI
(abridged)

Allegro amoroso

D♭ Major

BÖHME

BAGANTZ

Moderato

B♭ Minor

BÖHME

SCHERZO

BAGANTZ

Scherzo D. C. al Fine

B Major

BÖHME

Poco Andante (in 8)

BAGANTZ

Fine

D. C. al Fine

G# Minor

Andante con spirito

BAGANTZ

Tempo comodo

BÖHME

48

Gb Major

BÖHME

BAGANTZ

Allegro mosso

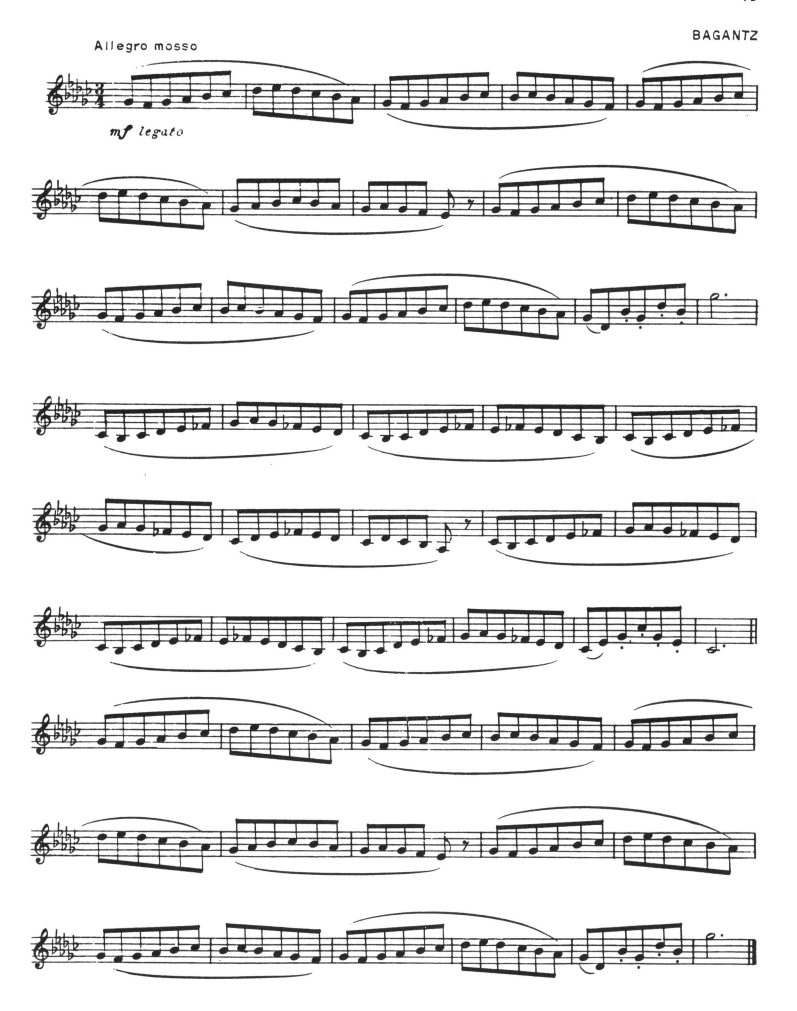

E♭ Minor

BÖHME

BAGANTZ

F♯ Major

DUHEM

GARIBALDI

Allegro brillante

D# Minor

FEDOROW

Allegro moderato

Fine

Meno allegro

con sentimento

D. C. al Fine

Scales

The use of a metronome with the following studies is highly recommended.

C Major

A Minor (melodic form)★

F Major

D Minor

★ All minor scale exercises should also be practiced in the harmonic form.

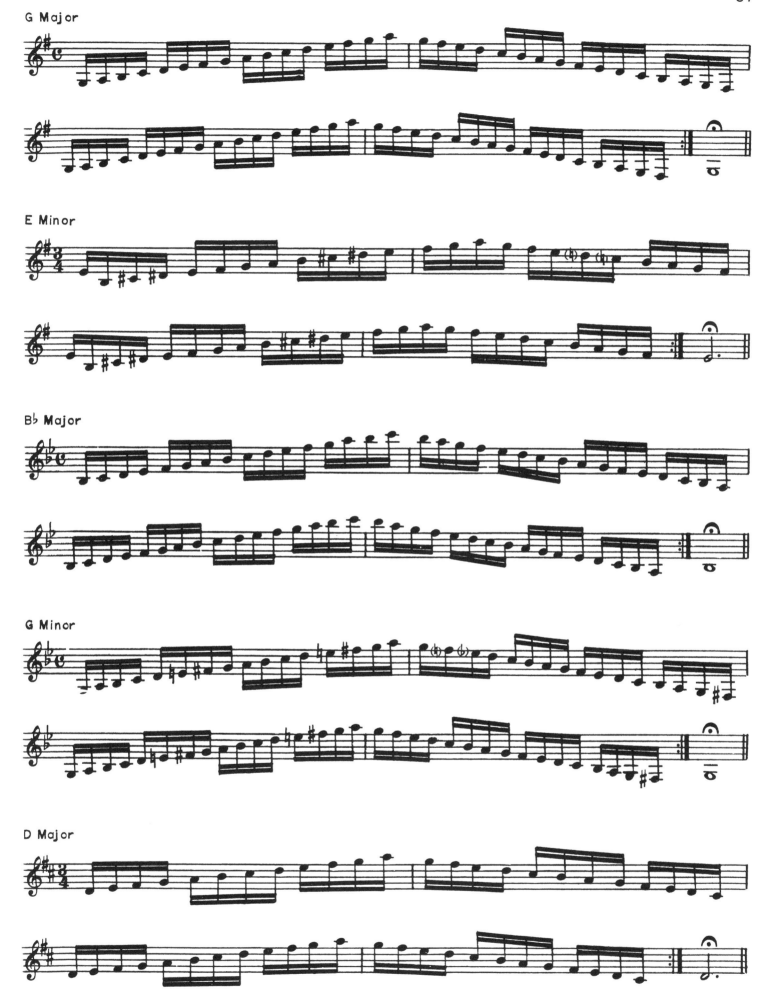

G Major

E Minor

B♭ Major

G Minor

D Major

B Minor

Eb Major

C Minor

A Major

F# Minor

60

Bb Minor

B Major

G# Minor

Gb Major

Eb Minor

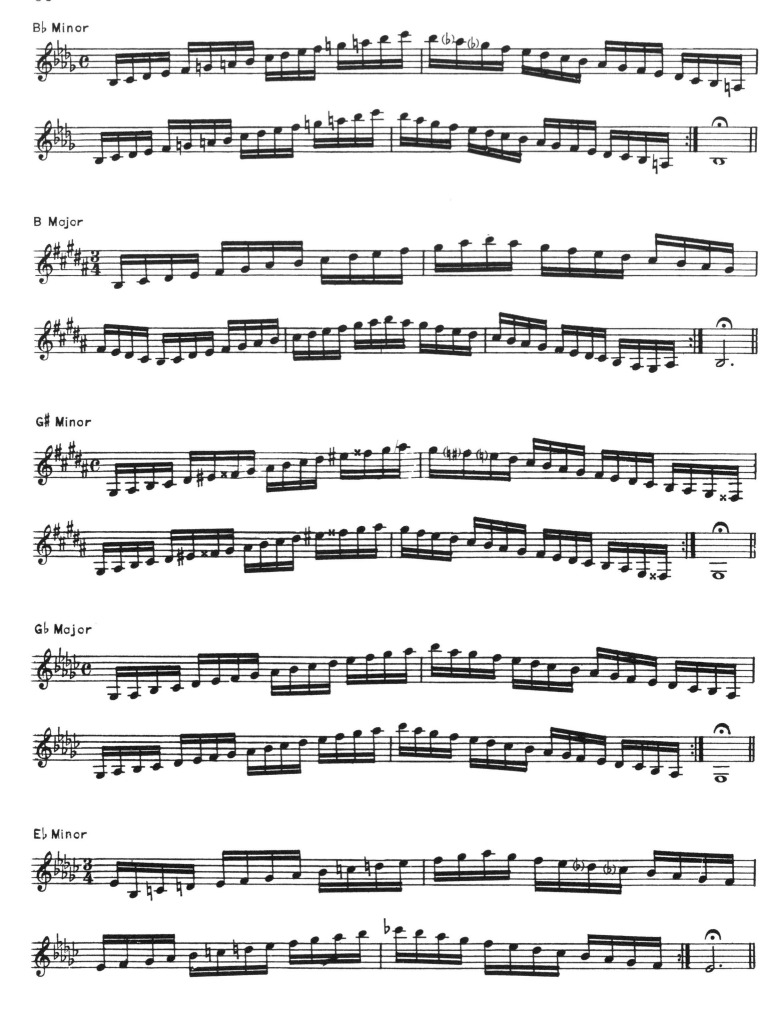

F# Major

D# Minor

Whole-tone scale on F#.

Whole-tone scale on G.

Chromatic scales.

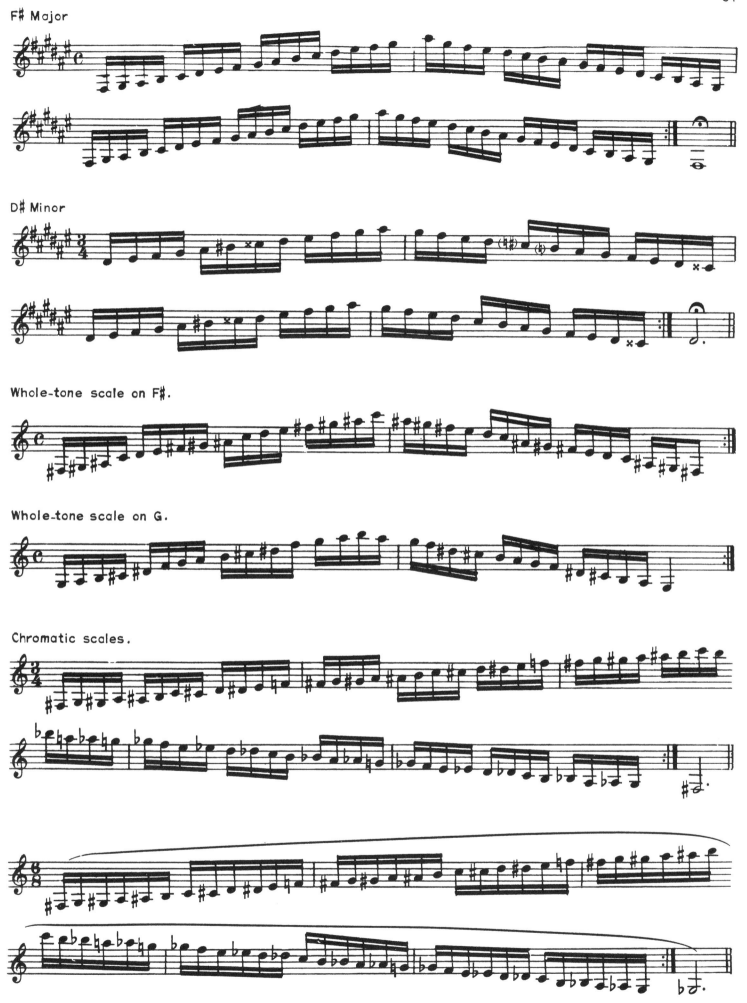

Chromatic Study

Practice with various articulations.

Interval Studies

BAGANTZ

ARBAN

ARBAN

ARBAN

Mosso

Arpeggios

70

Db Major

Bb Minor

B Major

G# Minor

Gb Major

Eb Minor

F# Major

D# Minor

Arpeggio of the augmented 5th.

Velocity

ST. JACOME
(adapted)

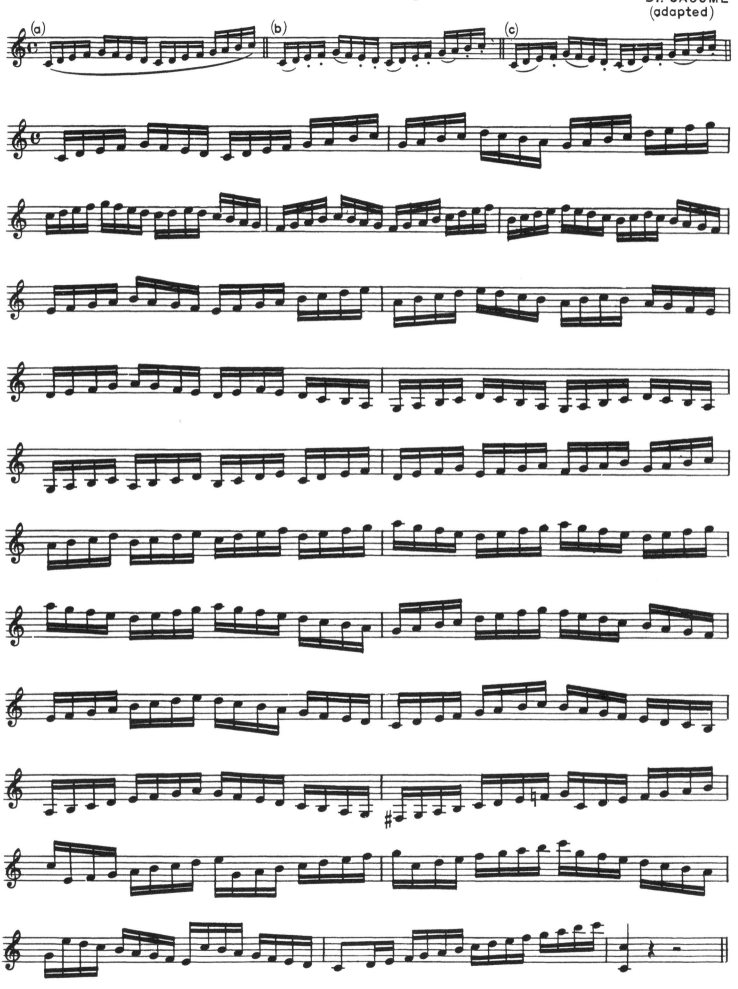

Allegro ma non troppo
Single and double tonguing.

CHAVANNE

NOTE: (♪) to be slighted or omitted if necessary when taking breath.

Allegro moderato

CHAVANNE

Single and triple tonguing.

Cadenza Studies